Managing Editor
Ina Massler Levin, M.A.

Editor
Eric Migliaccio

Contributing Editors
Sarah Smith
Kristine Smith

Creative Director
Karen J. Goldfluss, M.S. Ed.

Cover Design
Tony Carrillo / Marilyn Goldberg

Teacher Created Resources
12621 Western Avenue
Garden Grove, CA 92841
www.teachercreated.com

ISBN: 978-1-4206-5965-8

©2007 Teacher Created Resources
Reprinted, 2025 (PO606073)

Made in U.S.A.

This book belongs to

____

Get Ready to Learn!

Get ready, get set, and go! Boost your child's learning with this exciting series of books. Geared to help children practice and master many needed skills, the *Ready·Set·Learn* books are bursting with 64 pages of learning fun. Use these books for . . .

- enrichment
- skills reinforcement
- extra practice

With their smaller size, the *Ready·Set·Learn* books fit easily in children's hands, backpacks, and book bags. All your child needs to get started are pencils, crayons, and colored pencils.

A full sheet of colorful stickers is included. Use these stickers for . . .

- decorating pages
- rewarding outstanding effort
- keeping track of completed pages

Celebrate your child's progress by using these stickers on the reward chart located on the inside cover. The blue-ribbon sticker fits perfectly on the certificate on page 64.

With *Ready·Set·Learn* and a little encouragement, your child will be on the fast track to learning fun!

Pattern Time

Directions: Look at each pattern. Choose the picture that comes next from the box with the diagonal line. Color the picture that comes next.

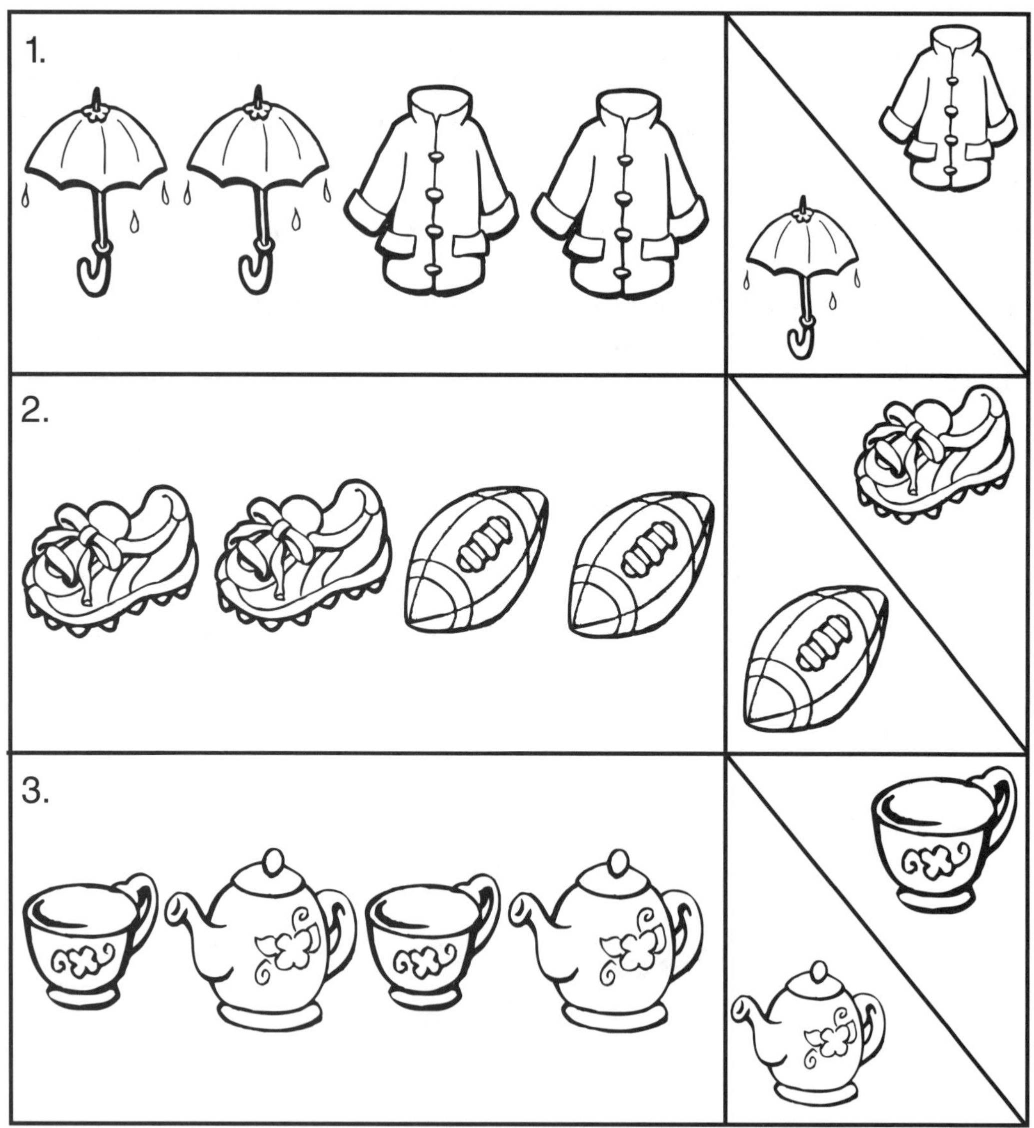

Plenty of Patterns

Directions: Look at each pattern. Choose the picture in the box with diagonal line that comes next in the pattern. Circle that picture.

Sports Patterns

Directions: Color each pattern. Complete each pattern by coloring the picture that comes next in the pattern.

1. 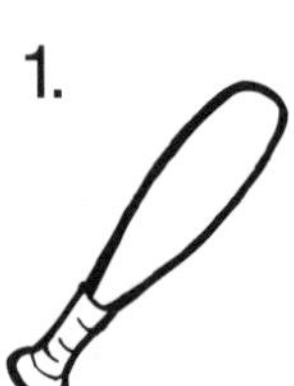    

2.     

3.     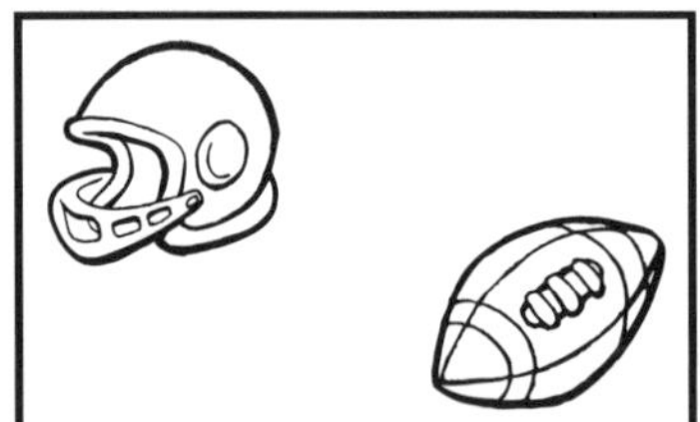

4.     

Hey Diddle, Diddle

Directions: Circle the object at the end of the row that finishes the pattern.

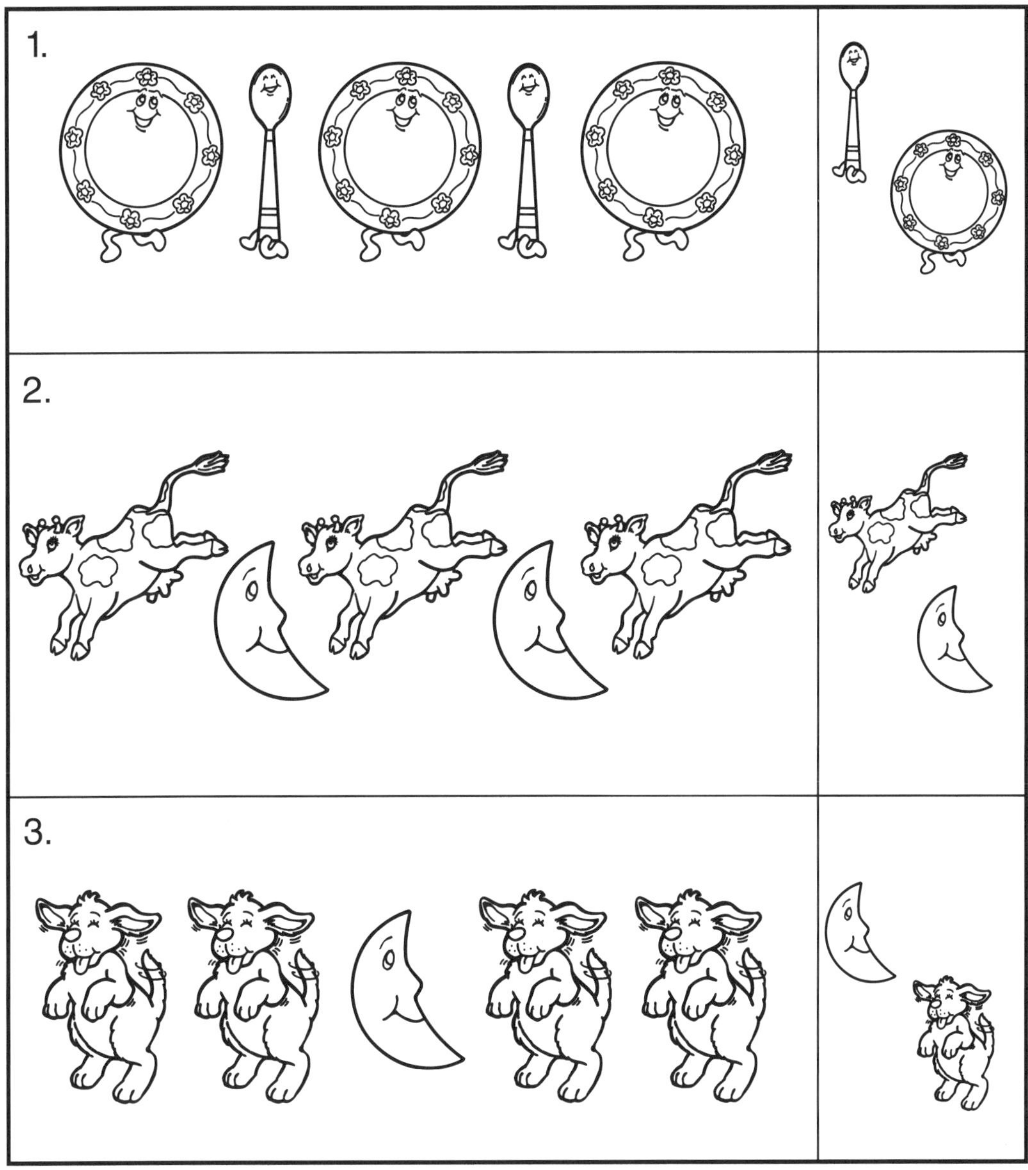

Finish the Pattern

Directions: Color each pattern. Complete each pattern by coloring the picture that will come next.

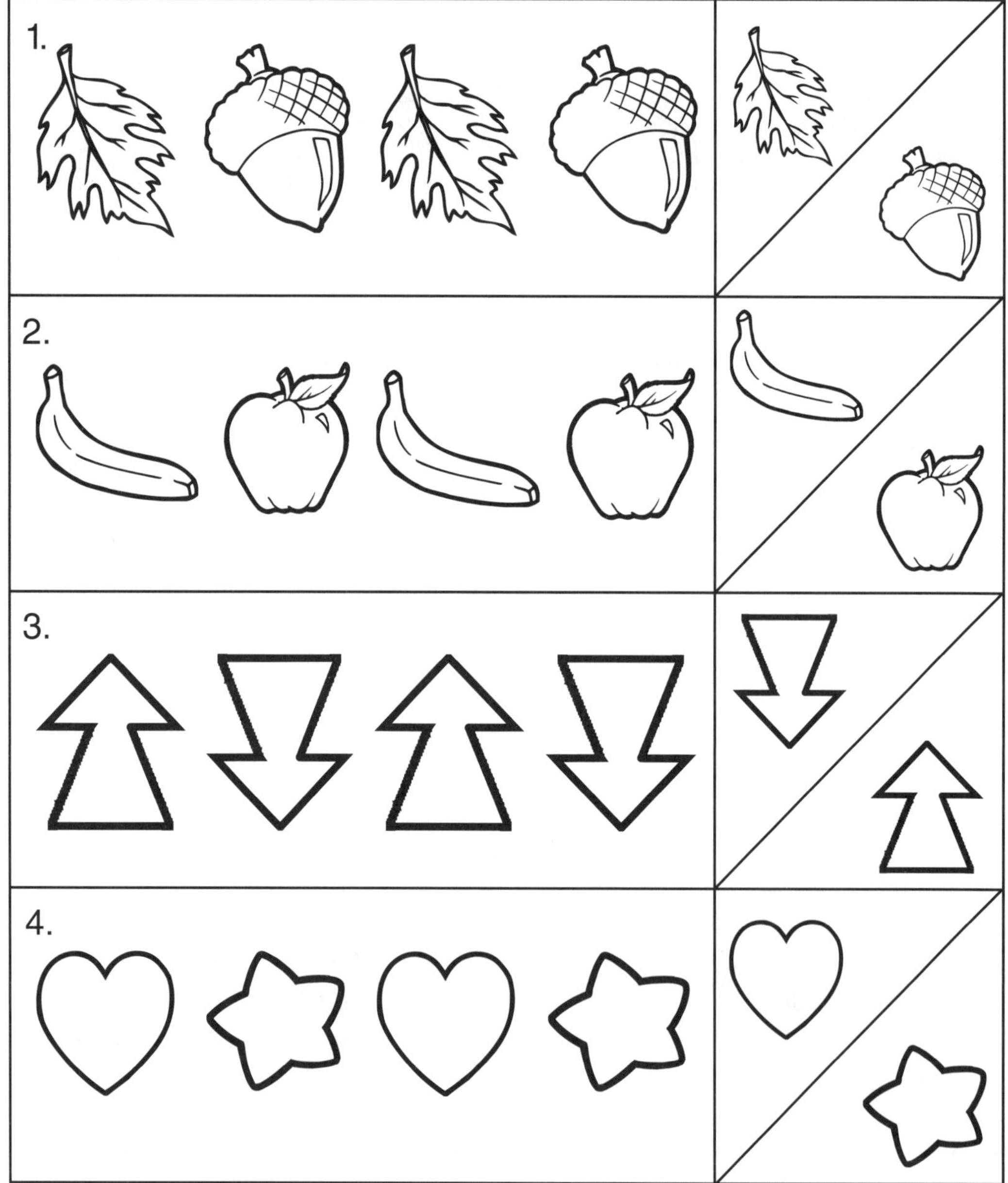

Extend the Pattern

Directions: Extend the patterns below by drawing the correct shapes.

1.

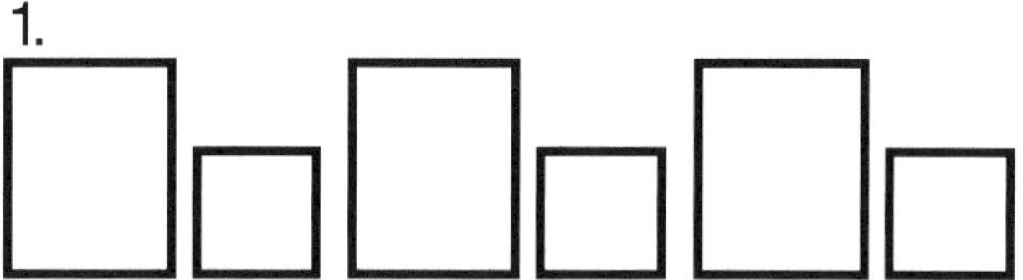

______ ______

2.

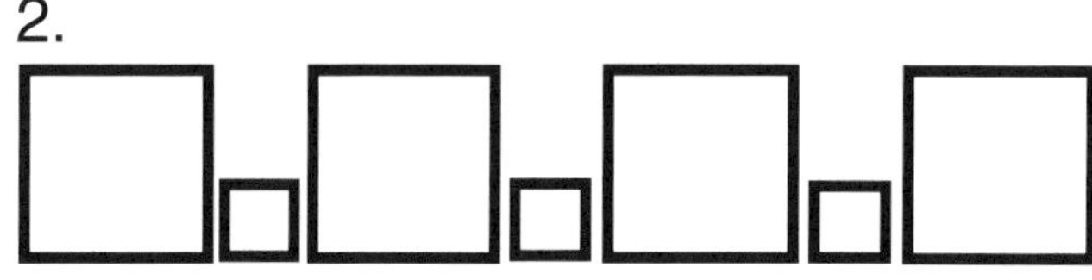

______ ______

3.

______ ______

4.

______ ______

5.

______ ______

What Comes Next?

Directions: Look at the pattern in each row. Complete the pattern by drawing what comes next.

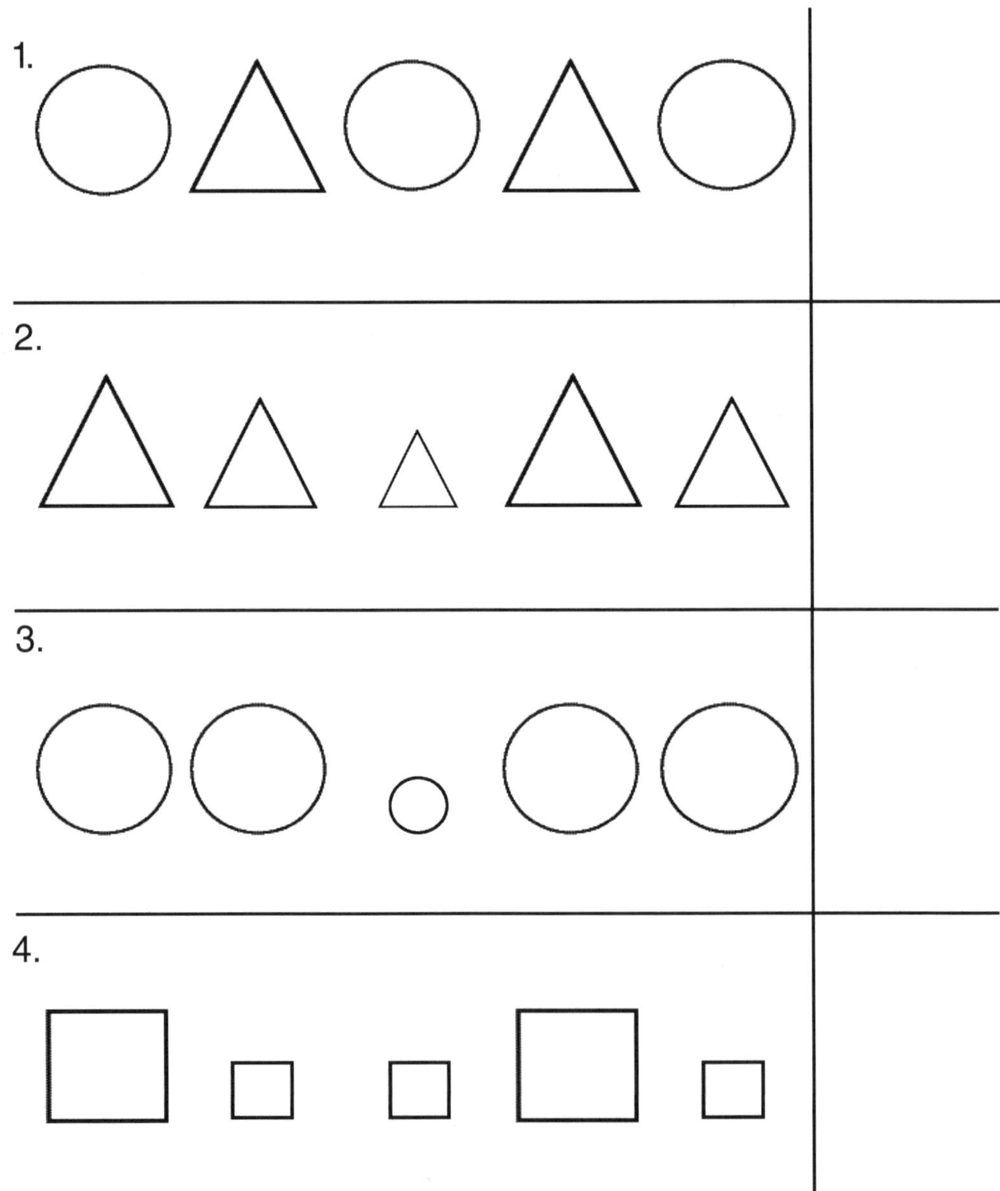

What Comes First?

Directions: Look at the patterns in each row. Complete the pattern by drawing what comes first.

1.

2.

3.

4.

Square Pattern

Directions: Look at the boxes. A pattern has been started. Choose a color and finish the pattern by coloring the appropriate squares. Color over the gray boxes, if you wish.

Triangle Pattern

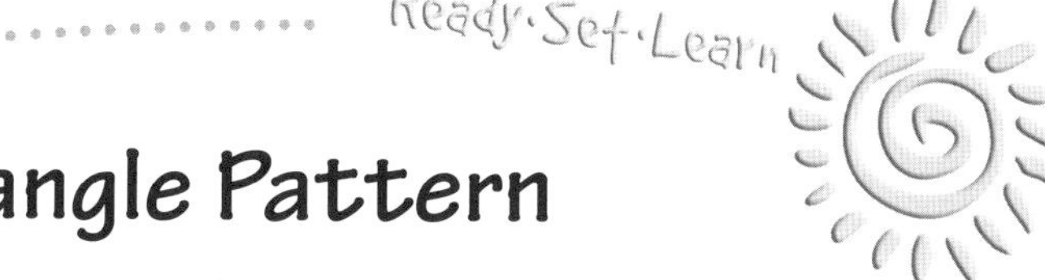

Directions: Look at the triangles below. A pattern has been started. Finish the pattern by coloring the appropriate triangles. Color over the gray triangles, if you wish.

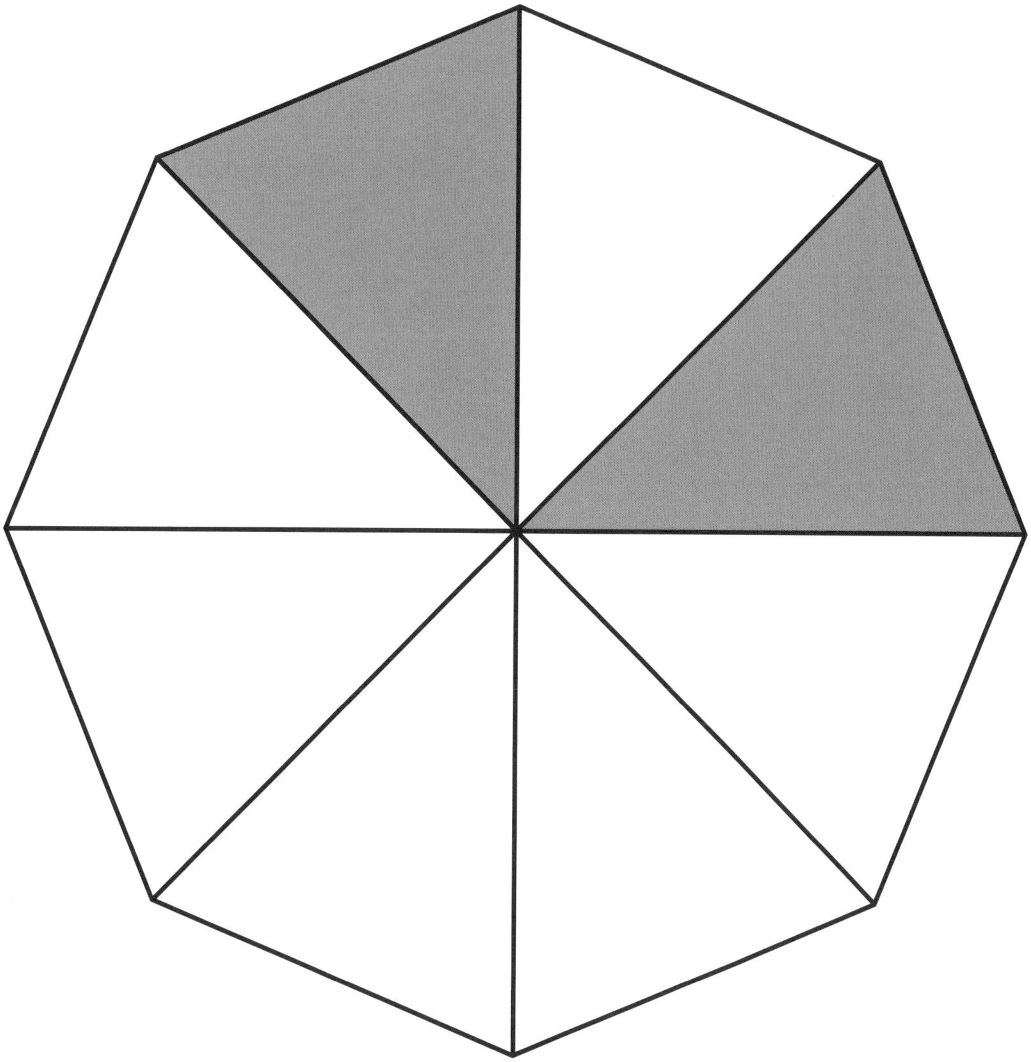

Flag Pattern

Directions: Use two colors to create a pattern on the flag.

Flag Patterns

Directions: Flags often have patterns of color. Color each flag, creating a pattern on each one.

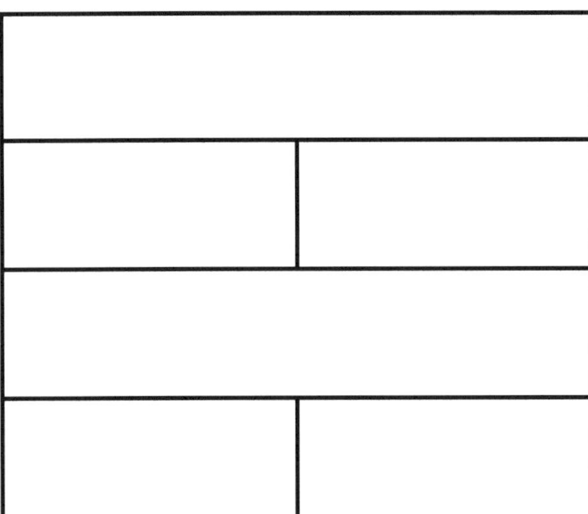

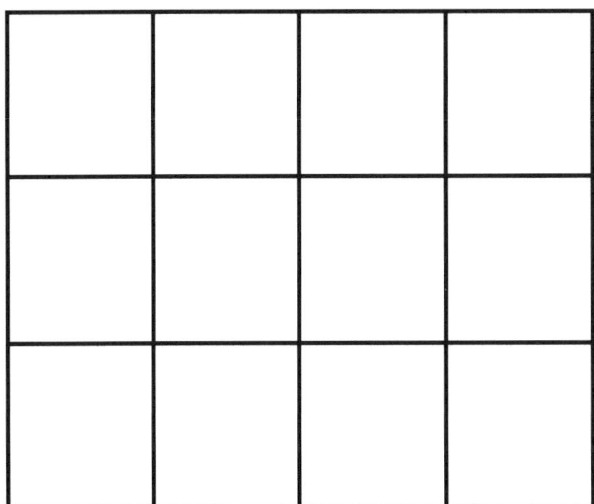

Stripey Shirts

Directions: Create a pattern on each shirt below. Use two or more colors on each shirt.

16

Finding Patterns

Directions: Find patterns in the picture. Color the patterns.

The Pattern Path

Directions: Help the lost girl find her way through the woods by following the path with a pattern of leaves and acorns.

Color Word Patterns

Directions: Read each color word. Color the necklaces following the color pattern.

1.

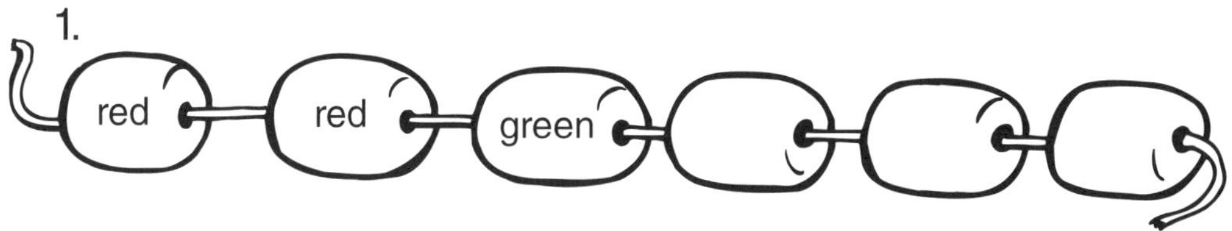

2.

3.

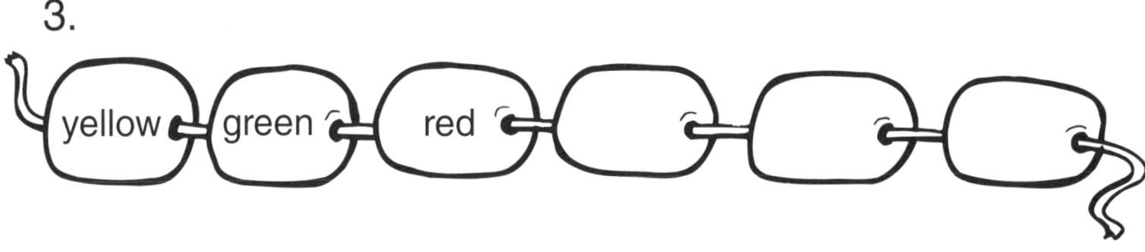

4.

Shape Beads

Directions: Finish each necklace by adding the correct shapes to continue the pattern. Color the necklaces.

1.

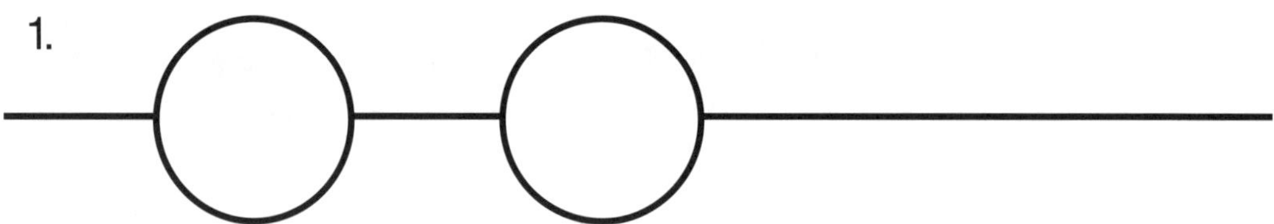

2.

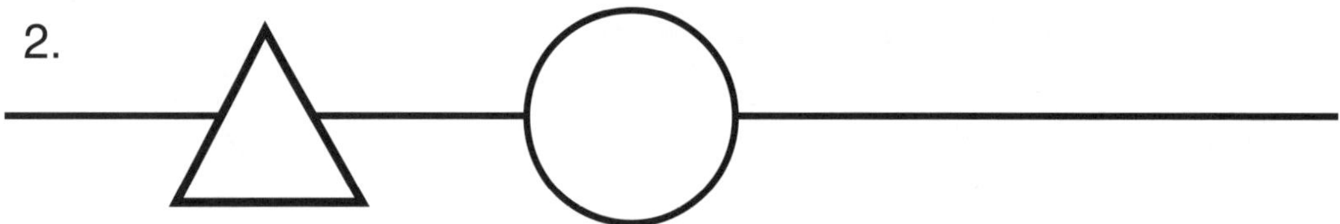

3.

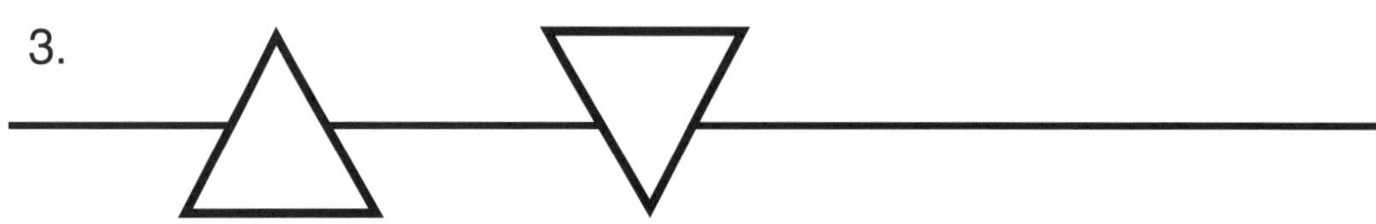

4.

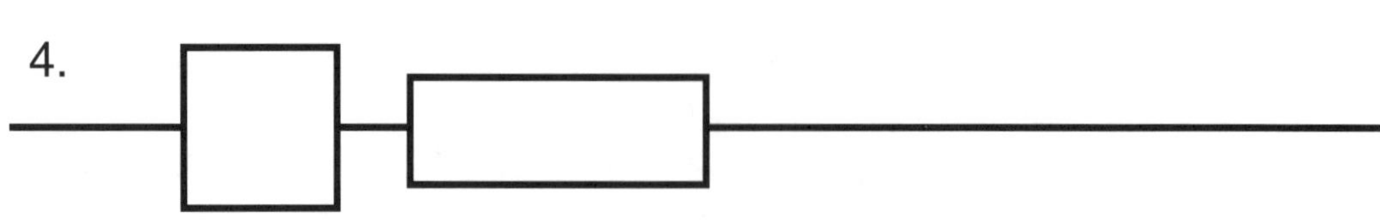

Colorful Beads

Directions: Continue each pattern. Color the beads.

1. 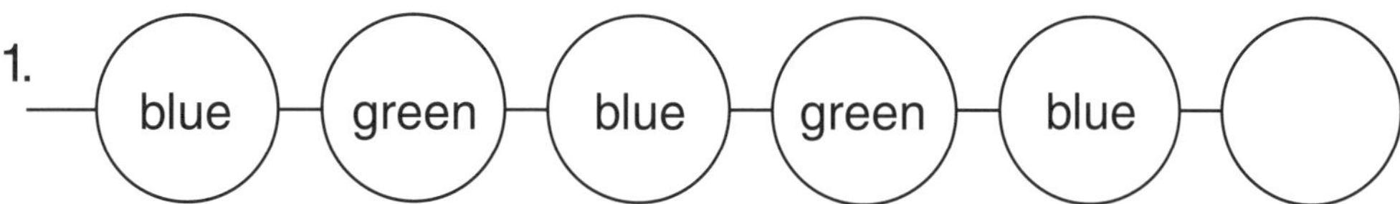

2. 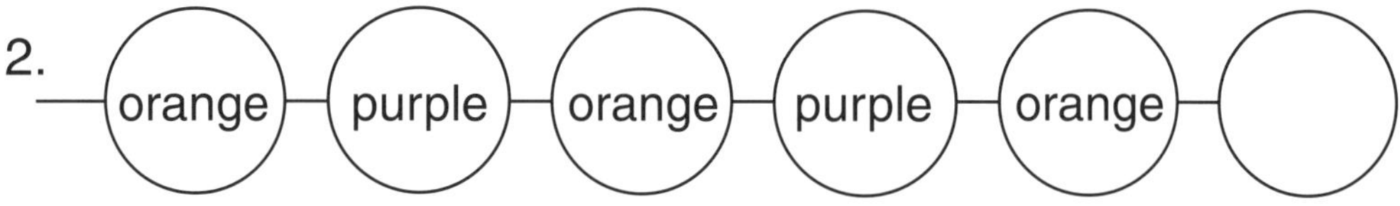

3. 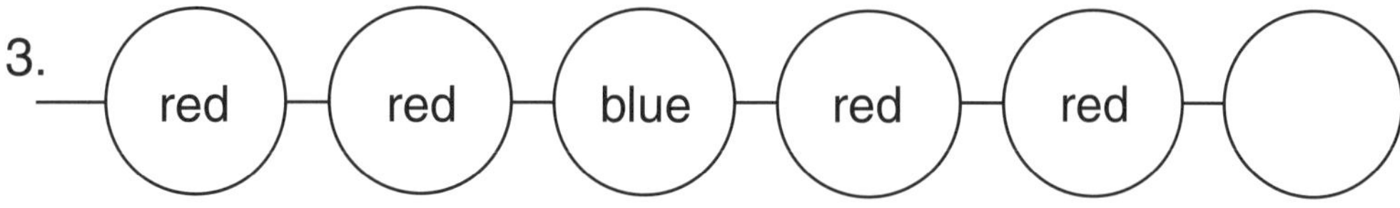

4. 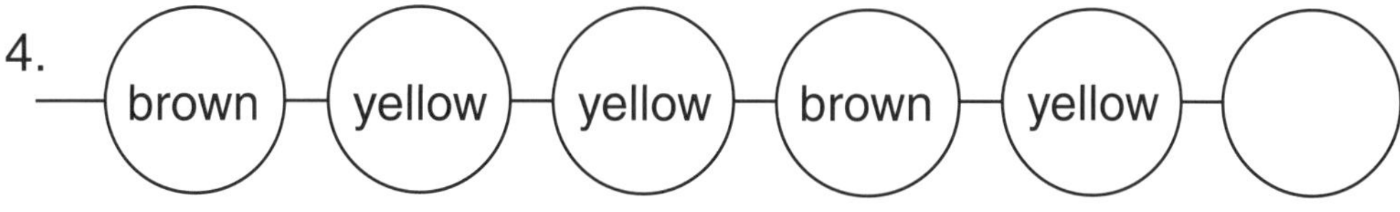

Number Patterns

Directions: Look at each line of number patterns. Write the missing number on each line to complete the pattern.

1. 0 1 0 1 0 ___

2. 6 7 8 ___ 7 8

3. 3 ___ 4 3 4 4

4. 9 8 7 9 ___ 7

5. ___ 2 3 1 2 3

Number Patterns

Directions: Look at each line of number patterns. Write the missing number on each line to complete the pattern.

1. 5 6 ___ 5 6 7

2. 6 ___ 4 3 ___ 1

3. 2 4 ___ 8 10 12

4. 3 4 5 ___ ___ 8

5. 10 8 6 ___ 2 0

Create a Pattern

Directions: Color the shapes below to create a pattern.
The first one has been started for you.

1.

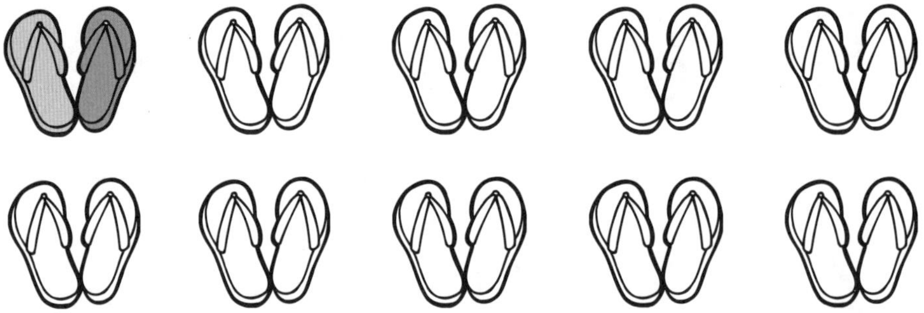

2.

3.

Which Pattern?

Directions: Look at the pattern in each row. Draw what comes next in the pattern.

1.	
2.	
3.	
4.	

How Many Candles?

Directions: Look at the cakes in each row. Count the candles on each cake to find a pattern. Draw in the missing number of candles on the last cake in each row.

1.

2.

3.

4.

Dots All Around

Directions: Look at the ladybugs in each row. Count the spots on each ladybug to find a pattern. Draw in the missing number of spots on the last ladybug in each row.

1.

2.

3.

4.

Shady Shapes

Directions: Look at the patterns of shapes in each row.
Complete each pattern by circling the shape that comes next.

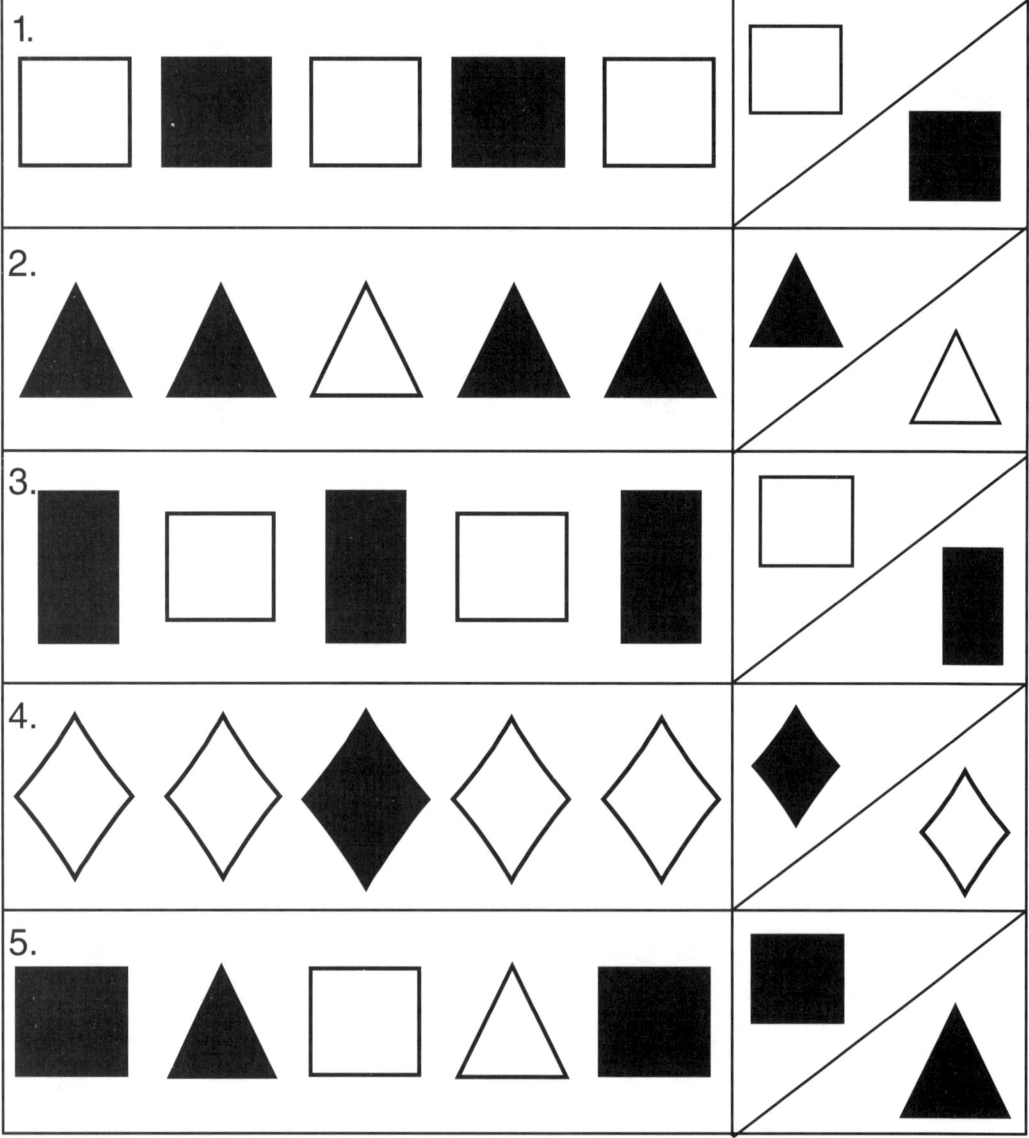

More Shady Shapes

Directions: Look at the patterns of shapes in each row. Complete each pattern by circling the shape that comes next.

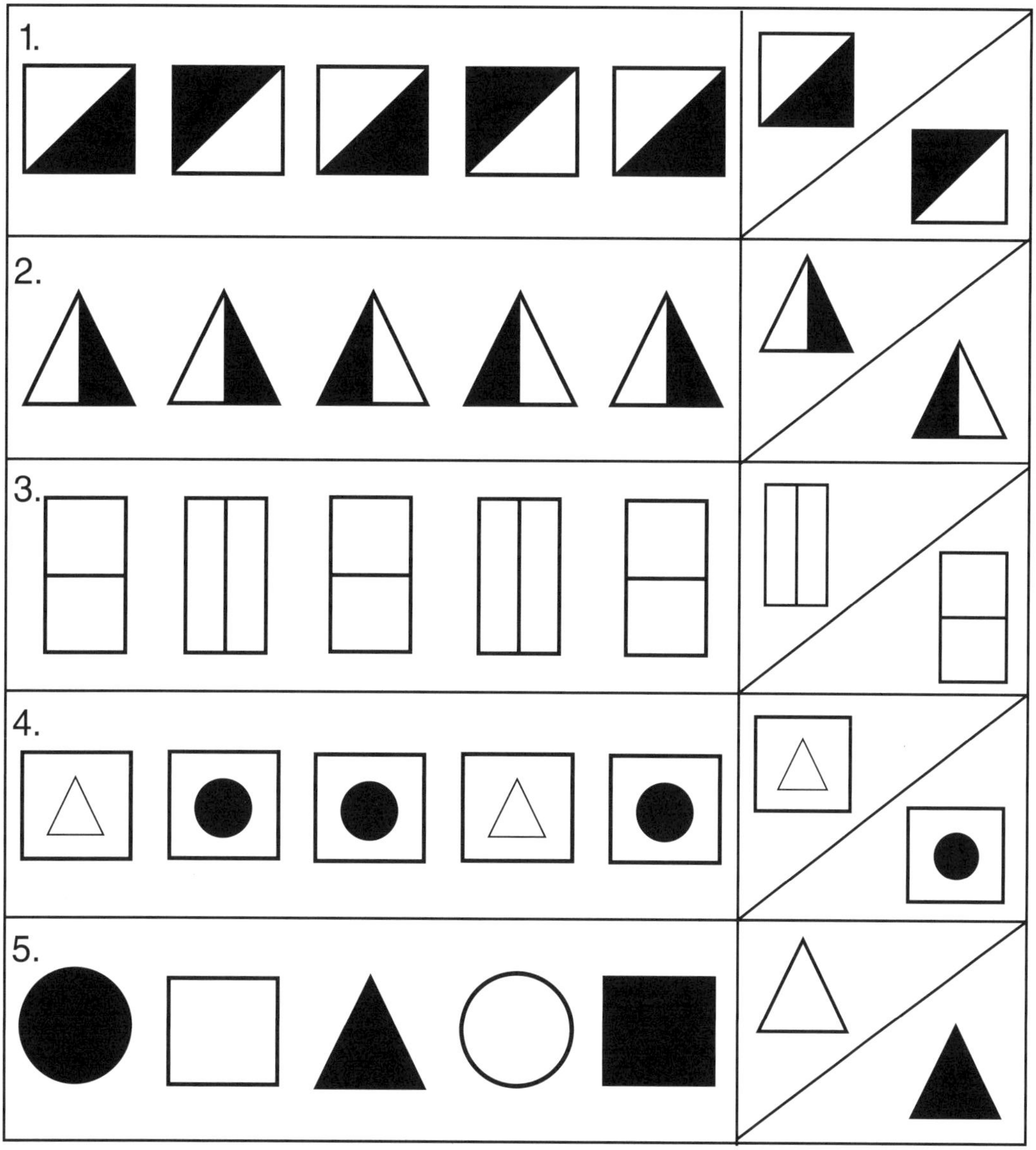

1.

2.

3.

4.

5.

Alphabet Sequencing

Directions: Each caterpillar shows a different list of letters
Write the missing capital letters to complete each list.

1. A B _ D _ F

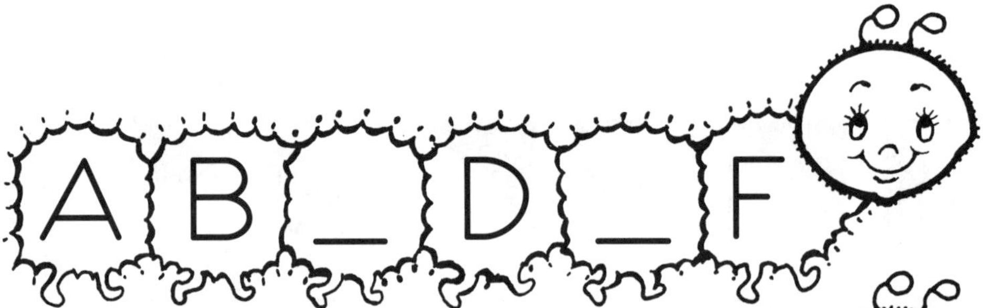

2. E _ _ _ H I _

3. J K _ M _ O

4. P _ _ R S _ _ _

Alphabet Train

Directions: Each train shows a different list of letters. Write the missing lowercase letters to complete each list.

1. a b ___ d

2. w ___ y ___

3. l m ___ ___

4. g ___ ___ j

5. r ___ ___ u

Alphabet Books

Directions: Each book should have a matching capital and lowercase letter on it. Write the missing capital or lowercase letter on each book. The first one is done for you.

Fill in the Letters

Directions: Write the missing lowercase letters to complete each list.

1. a b c ___ ___

2. l m n ___ ___

3. r s t ___ ___

4. f g h ___ ___

5. u v w ___ ___

Fill in More Letters

Directions: Write the missing lowercase letters to complete each list.

1. ___ ___ h i j

2. ___ ___ x y z

3. ___ ___ c d e

4. ___ ___ n o p

5. ___ ___ s t u

Picture Sequence

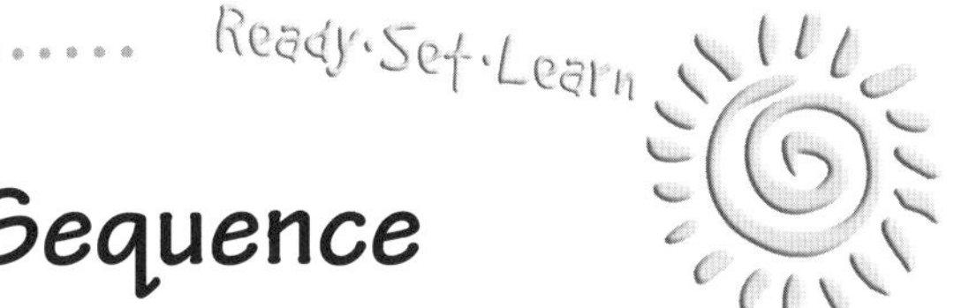

Directions: Put the pictures in each row in the correct order by writing **1**, **2**, or **3** on the line provided.

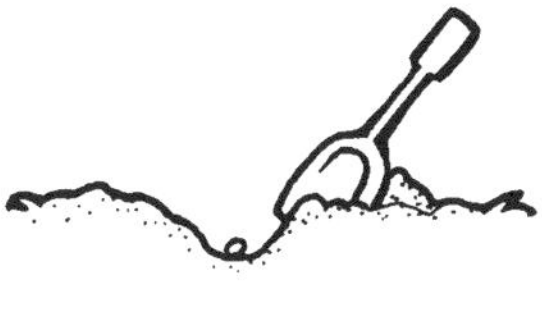

Growing and Changing

Directions: Look at the pictures in each row.
Write a **1** under the picture that shows the **beginning**.
Write a **2** under the picture that shows the **middle**.
Write a **3** under the picture that shows the **end**.

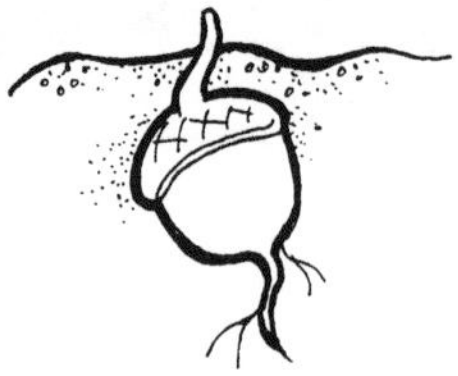

Trophy Time

Directions: Draw a line from each trophy to its matching ribbon.

Ordinal Numbers

Directions: Draw a line to match each pair of ordinal numbers.

1st	third
2nd	fifth
3rd	first
4th	fourth
5th	second

More Ordinal Numbers

Directions: Draw a line to match each pair of ordinal numbers.

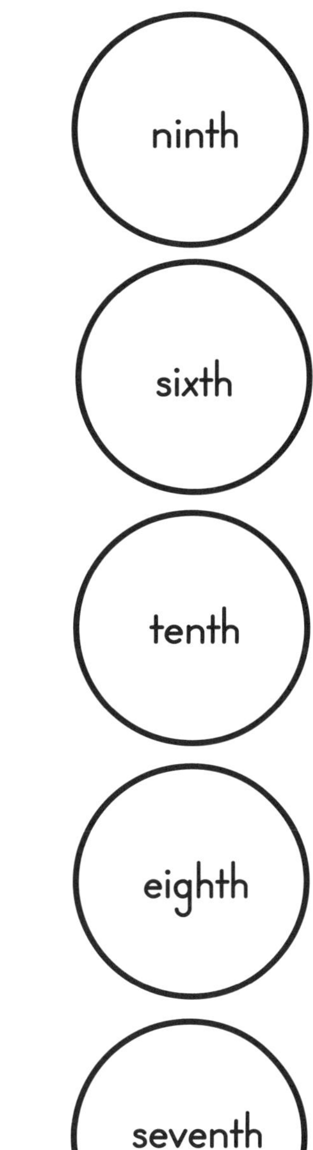

6th	ninth
7th	sixth
8th	tenth
9th	eighth
10th	seventh

Prized Animals

Directions: Look at the pictures in each row. Each animal got a ribbon that shows whether it won **first**, **second**, or **third** prize. Write **first**, **second**, or **third** under each picture to match the ribbon.

______________   ______________   ______________

______________   ______________   ______________

Set the Table

Directions: Write numbers in the boxes to show which picture comes first, second, third, and fourth.

Making Things

Directions: Look at the pictures in each row. Circle the word
First, **Second**, or **Third** under each picture.

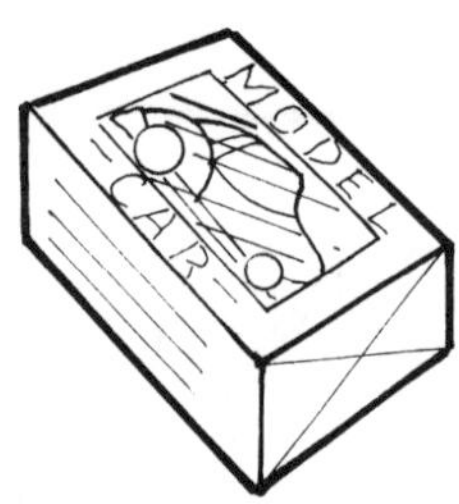

First
Second
Third

First
Second
Third

First
Second
Third

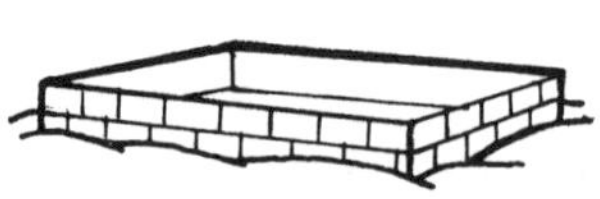

First
Second
Third

First
Second
Third

First
Second
Third

42

Making More Things

Directions: Write an **F** for **first**, an **S** for **second**, and a **T** for **third** under each picture.

Getting Dressed

Directions: Write numbers in the boxes to show which picture comes **first**, **second**, **third**, **fourth**, **fifth**, and **sixth**.

Snowman

Directions: Write numbers in the boxes to show which picture comes **first**, **second**, **third**, **fourth**, **fifth,** and **sixth**.

Food for Thought

Directions: Write a **B** under the picture that shows what happened in the **beginning**. Write an **M** under the picture that shows what happened in the **middle**. Write an **E** under the picture that shows what happened in the **end**.

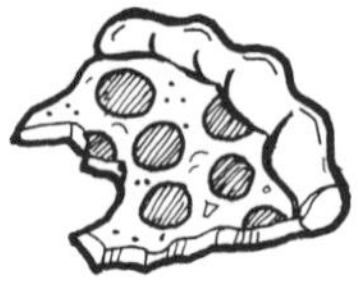

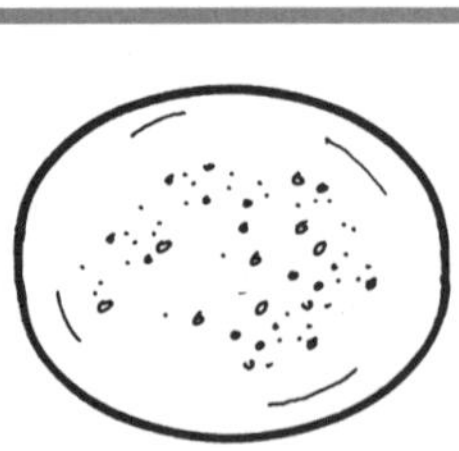

Getting Ready for Bed

Directions: Look at the three pictures in each row. Circle the word **Beginning**, **Middle**, or **End** under each picture.

Beginning Middle End

Beginning Middle End

Beginning Middle End

Beginning Middle End

Beginning Middle End

Beginning Middle End

Beginning Middle End

Beginning Middle End

Beginning Middle End

Life Cycles

Directions: Circle the **beginning** of each life cycle with a red crayon. Circle the **middle** of each life cycle with a green crayon. Circle the **end** of each life cycle with a blue crayon.

Life Cycle of a Butterfly

Life Cycle of a Frog

Life Cycle of a Chicken

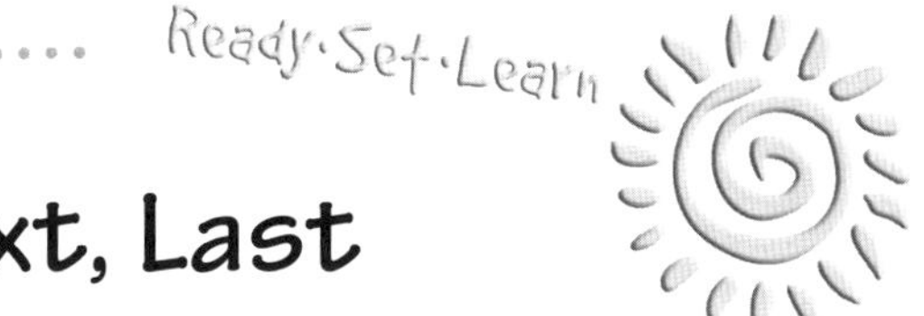

First, Next, Last

Directions: Number the events **1**, **2**, or **3** showing the order in each row of pictures.

What Comes Next?

Directions: Look at the sequence in each row. Look at the two boxes at the end of each row. Circle the picture that comes next in the sequence.

1.

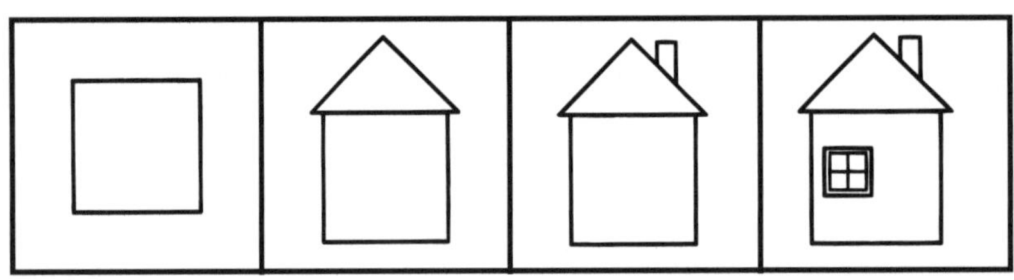 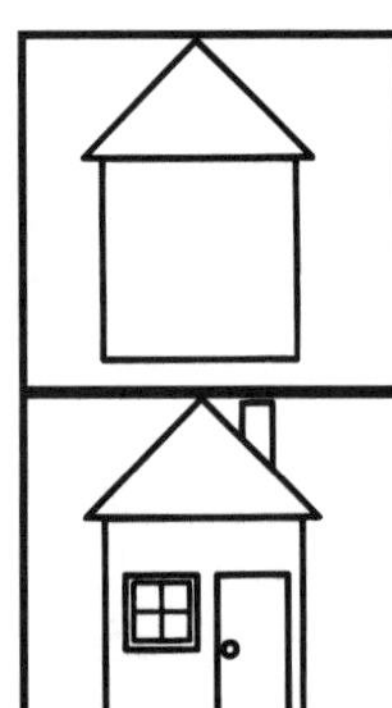

2.

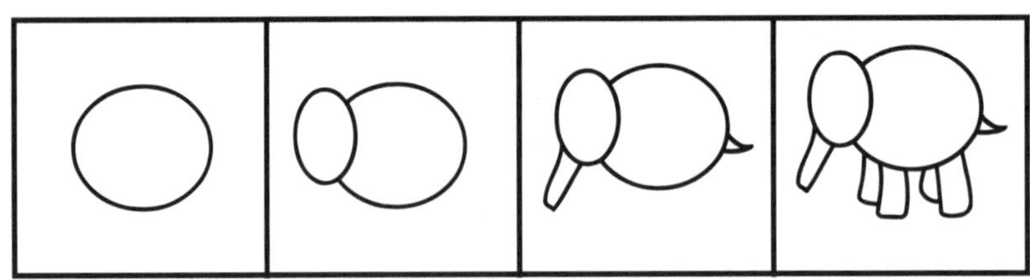 

3.

Before and After Numbers

Directions: Write the numbers that come before and after the given number.

1. ___ , 3 , ___	6. ___ , 17 , ___
2. ___ , 8 , ___	7. ___ , 23 , ___
3. ___ , 5 , ___	8. ___ , 15 , ___
4. ___ , 19 , ___	9. ___ , 10 , ___
5. ___ , 27 , ___	10. ___ , 20 , ___

Before and After Letters

Directions: Write the letters that come **before** and **after** the given letter.

1. ___, P, ___	6. ___, H, ___
2. ___, J, ___	7. ___, B, ___
3. ___, C, ___	8. ___, X, ___
4. ___, G, ___	9. ___, T, ___
5. ___, Q, ___	10. ___, O, ___

In the Middle

Directions: Write the numbers and letters that come in between the numbers and letters given.

1. 5, ___, 7	6. C, ___, E
2. 12, ___, 14	7. M, ___, O
3. 8, ___, 6	8. V, ___, X
4. 15, ___, 17	9. H, ___, J
5. 2, ___, 6	10. O, ___, Q

Small to Big

Directions: Put the gifts in order from smallest to biggest by drawing a line from each gift to the number that shows the order. (smallest = 1; largest = 4)

Fire Safety
Stop, Drop, and Roll

Directions: Put the stop, drop, and roll pictures in the correct order. Write the number under the picture.

____

_______________   _______________

Before and After 1

Directions: The pictures on the left side of the page show what happened **before** the pictures on the right side of the page.
Draw a line to connect the **Before** picture on the left side with its **After** picture on the right side.

Before and After 2

Directions: Look at the three pictures in each row. Circle the **happy face** or **sad face** to tell how you would feel **before** and **after** the event shown in the middle of each row.

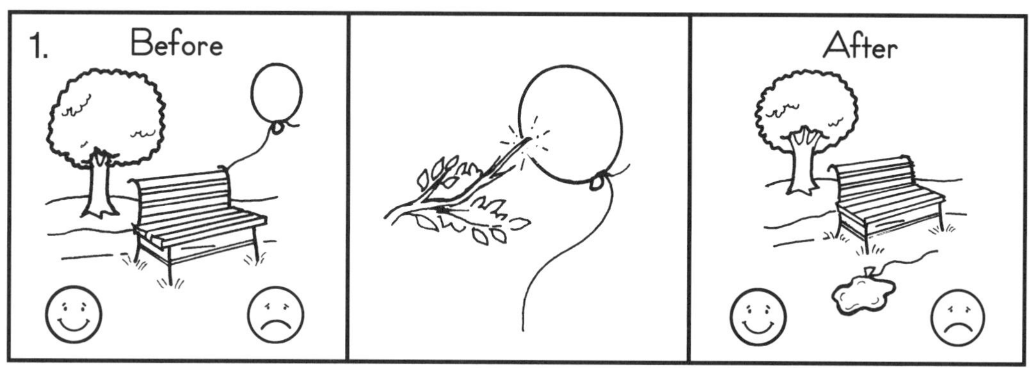

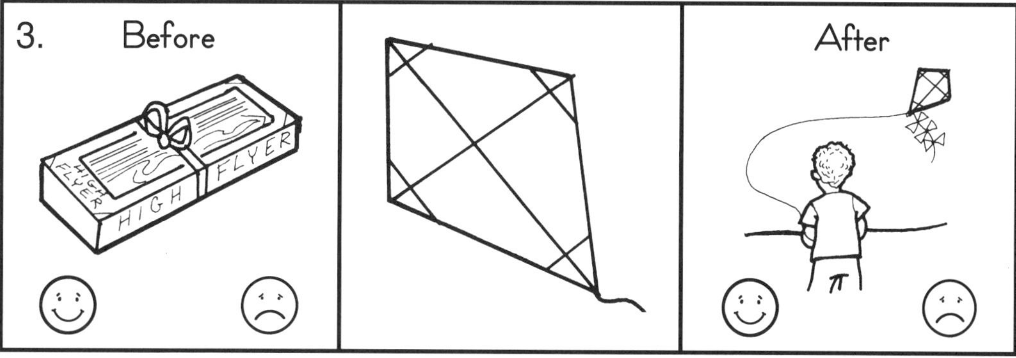

Before and After 3

Directions: Look at each pair of pictures. Decide if the first picture comes **before** or **after** the second picture. Circle **Before** or **After** under each picture to show the correct order.

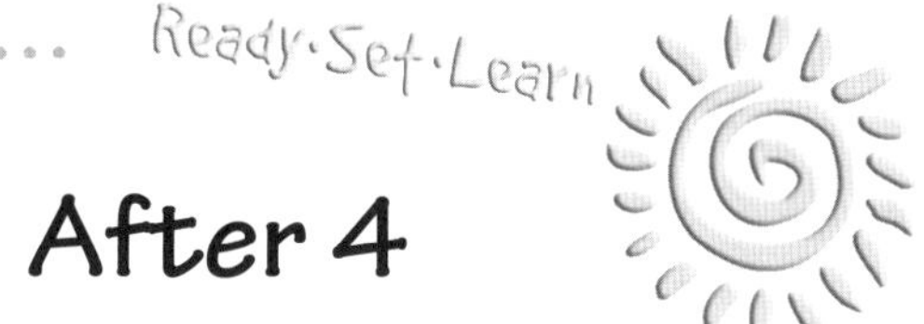

Before and After 4

Directions: Look at each pair of pictures. In each box, write a **1** under the picture that comes **before** you clean up. Then write a **2** under the picture that comes **after** you clean up.

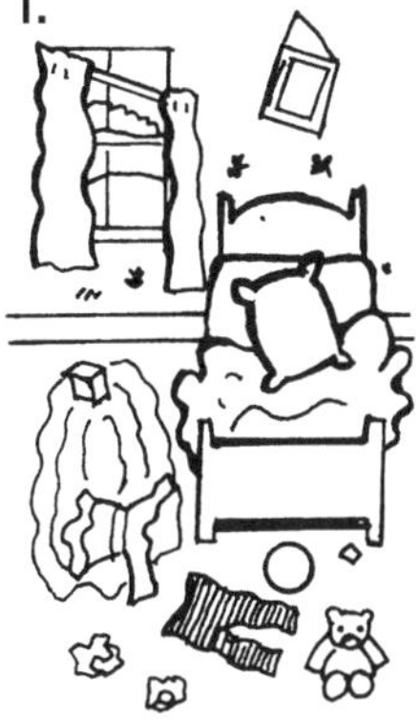

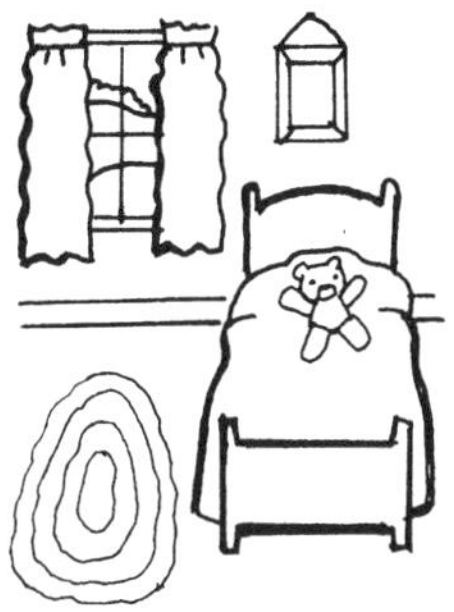

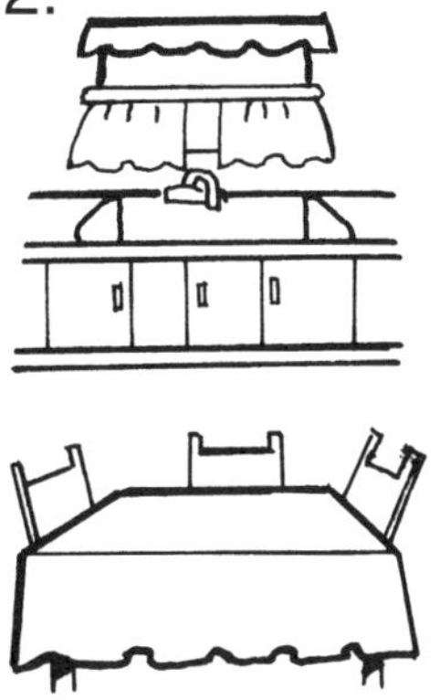

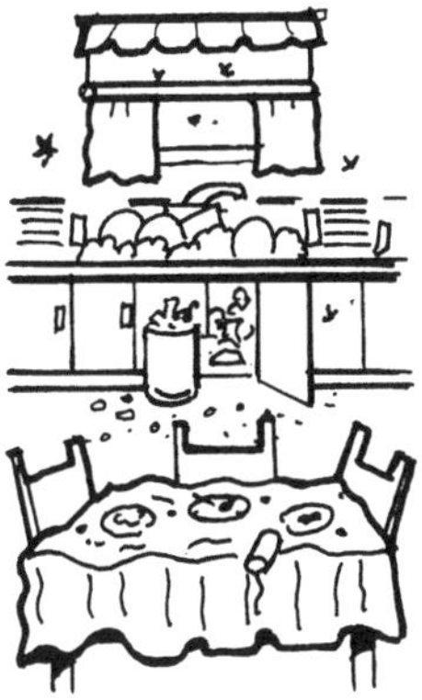

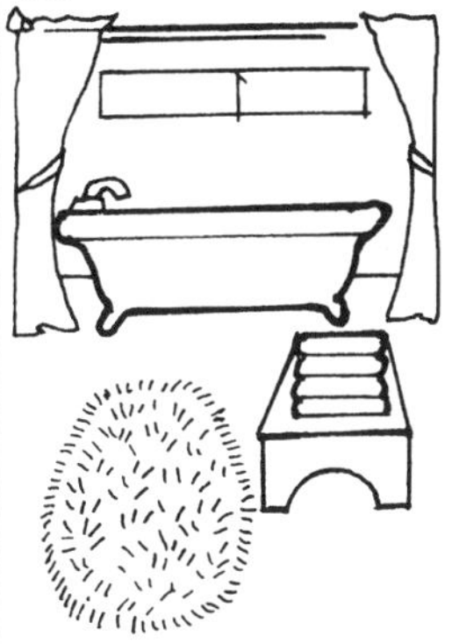

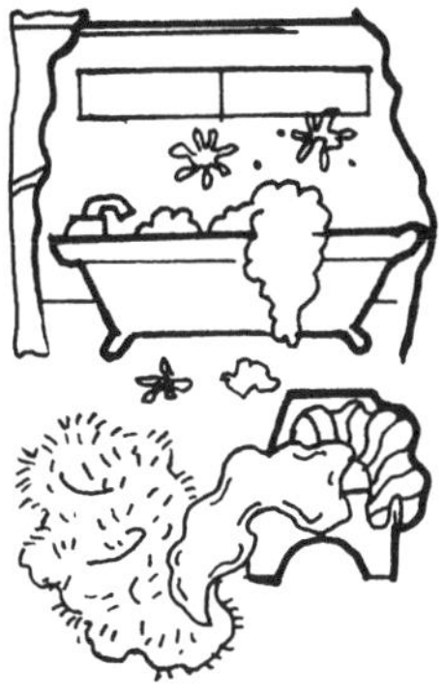

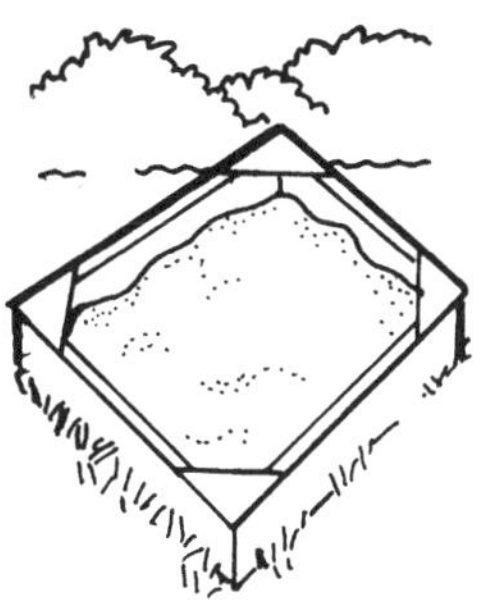

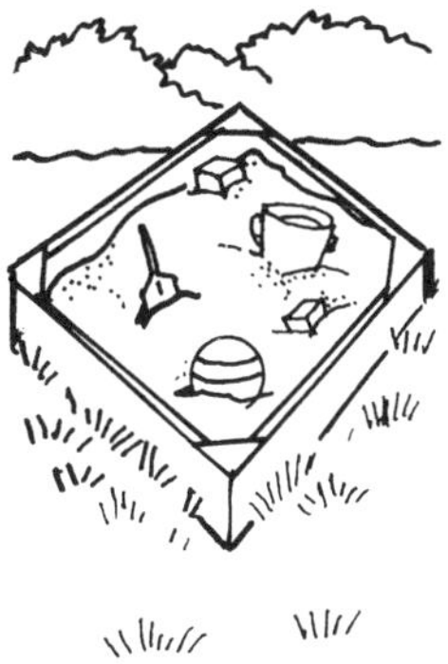

Answer Key

Page 4
1. umbrella
2. shoe
3. cup

Page 5
1. frog
2. barn
3. mailbox

Page 6
1. bat
2. shirt
3. helmet
4. hoop

Page 7
1. spoon
2. moon
3. moon

Page 8
1. leaf
2. banana
3. up arrow
4. heart

Page 9
1. rectangle, square
2. small square, big square
3. small circle, triangle
4. medium heart, small heart
5. up triangle, down triangle

Page 10
1. triangle
2. small triangle
3. small circle
4. small square

Page 11
1. circle
2. small triangle
3. big circle
4. up triangle

Pages 12–13
Students should continue the pattern.

Page 14–17
Answers will vary.

Page 18

Pages 19–20
Students should continue the patterns.

Page 21
1. green
2. purple
3. blue
4. yellow

Page 22
1. 1
2. 6
3. 4
4. 8
5. 1

Page 23
1. 7
2. 5, 2
3. 6
4. 6, 7
5. 4

Page 24
Answers will vary.

Page 25
1. moon
2. circle
3. fish
4. banana

Page 26
1. 4 candles
2. 2 candles
3. 3 candles
4. 6 candles

Page 27
1. 4 dots

2. 9 dots
3. 12 dots
4. 8 dots

Page 28
1. black square
2. white triangle
3. white square
4. black diamond
5. black triangle

Page 29
1. ◤
2. ◮
3. ‖
4. ▣
5. △

Page 30
1. C, E
2. F, G, J
3. L, N
4. Q, T, U

Page 31
1. c
2. x, z
3. n, o
4. h, i
5. s, t

Page 32

B, C, d, e, F, G, h, I, j, K, l, m, N, o, P, q, R, S, t, u, v, W, x, Y, z

Page 33
1. d, e
2. o, p
3. u, v
4. i, j
5. x, y

Page 34
1. f, g
2. v, w
3. a, b
4. l, m
5. q, r

Page 35
first row: 1, 3, 2
second row: 2, 3, 1
third row: 3, 1, 2

Page 36
first row: 1, 3, 2
second row: 3, 2, 1
third row: 2, 1, 3

Page 37
first — 1st
second — 2nd
third — 3rd

Page 38
1st — first
2nd — second
3rd — third
4th — fourth
5th — fifth

Page 39
6th — sixth
7th — seventh
8th — eight
9th — ninth
10th — tenth

Page 40
first row: first, second, third
second row: third, first, second

Page 41
clockwise (from top left): 1, 4, 2, 3

Page 42
first row: first, third, second
second row: second, first, third

Page 43
first row: S, F, T
second row: T, S, F
third row: S, F, T

<h1 style="text-align:center">Answer Key (cont.)</h1>

Page 44

clockwise (from top left): 3, 4, 1, 5, 2, 6

Page 45

clockwise (from top left): 1, 5, 6, 2, 4, 3

Page 46

first row: M, E, B
second row: E, B, M
third row: B, E, M

Page 47

first row: End, Beginning, Middle
second row: Beginning, Middle, End
third row: Beginning, Middle, End

Page 48

first row: Middle, End, Beginning
second row: End, Middle, Beginning
third row: Middle, Beginning, End

Page 49

first row: 2, 3, 1
second row: 3, 1, 2
third row: 3, 1, 2

Page 50

1. complete house
2. complete elephant
3. complete face

Page 51

1. 2, 4
2. 7, 9
3. 4, 6
4. 18, 20
5. 26, 28
6. 16, 18
7. 22, 24
8. 14, 16
9. 9, 11
10. 19, 21

Page 52

1. O, Q
2. I, K
3. B, D
4. F, H
5. P, R
6. G, I

7. A, C
8. W, Y
9. S, U
10. N, P

Page 53

1. 6
2. 13
3. 7
4. 16
5. 4
6. D
7. N
8. W
9. I
10. P

Page 54

from smallest to biggest: dots, spots, stripes, hearts

Page 55

2, 1, 3

Page 56

Page 57

Answers will vary.

Page 58

1. before, after
2. before, after
3. after, before
4. after, before

Page 59

1. 1, 2
2. 2, 1
3. 2, 1
4. 2, 1

This Award
Is Presented To

____

for

★ Doing Your Best

★ Trying Hard

★ Not Giving Up

★ Making a
Great Effort